and there I was . . .

An adventure in historical fiction for creative young writers

Grades 4-9

by
Marji Gold-Vukson

illustrated by
Micheal Gold-Vukson

Blackline Masters

A gct Publication

Dedication

The year was 1894, and there I wasn't . . .
but Gussie London Gold was.

Happy 96th birthday, Grandma Gussie!
This one's for you . . .

Purchase of this book entitles the individual teacher to duplicate the materials herein for one class only. Absolutely no duplication of material for an entire school or school system is allowed.

ISBN 0-937659-40-1
©1990
GCT, Inc.
Printed in the United States of America

Table of Contents

Dear Teacher 2

Directions to the Student 3

A Few Hints 3

The Year was . . .

    1902: Rudyard Kipling's *Just So Stories* 4
    1903: The Wright Brothers' First Flight 6
    1909: Robert Edwin Peary's Expedition North 8
    1909: Henry Ford's Assembly Line 10
    1912: The Unsinkable Titanic 12
    1912: Hans Geiger's Radiation Detector 14
    1914: The Panama Canal — Open for Business 16
    1919: Mahatma Means Great Soul 18
    1920: Temperance 20
    1925: John Baird's T.V. 22
    1927: Charles Lindbergh's Nonstop Flight 24
    1929: Black Thursday 26
    1936: A Royal Love Story 28
    1939: Good as Mold 30
    1944: Anne Frank's Secret Place 32
    1945: Hiroshima and Nagasaki 34
    1947: A Sonic Boom 36
    1950: One for All and All for One — NATO 38
    1956: Deposit Another Dime, Please 40
    1958: Bobby Fischer and the Big Checkmate 42
    1960: J.F.K., the Nation's Youngest President 44
    1963: Valentina Tereshkova — Out of This World 46
    1968: Martin Luther King, Robert F. Kennedy 48
    1976: A Mysterious Illness — Legionnaires' Disease 50
    1978: A $2,000,000 Bible 52
    1978: The Return of Susan B. Anthony 54
    1982: A Heart Called Jarvik-7 56
    1986: Voyager II and the Ten New Moons 58
    1989: A Hero Named Secretariat 60

Dear Teacher,

Perhaps you selected this book because, as a professional educator, you understand the importance of *teaching history*, not the history that is just so many random dates and events, but the history that is the lives, times, accomplishments, emotions, and thoughts of real people. Perhaps you selected this book because you would like to afford your students many opportunities to become involved in *research*, exploring issues of the past and seeking answers about how these might impact upon the future. Maybe you selected this book to promote experience in *creative writing*, encouraging creative young people to draw upon actual events and their implications in the preparation of short stories. *And there I was . . .* is an adventure in historical fiction for creative young writers and, as such, incorporates each of these elements (history, research, and creative writing) into one book.

Historical fiction involves telling a story which has the feel for a selected time in the past. Because making the reader feel as if (s)he was "there" requires some effort, it is important for the young writers to become as familiar as possible with the selected historical period. This includes even seemingly insignificant details such as period clothing, technology, culture, popular names, popular lingo, and so on. Therefore, both an interest in history and a familiarity with research skills are necessary to the success of writing historical fiction.

You may find it helpful to offer your students the opportunity to explore some of the fine historical fiction that has been written for young people. Below are the titles of a few of the award-winning books they may enjoy.

Newbery Medal Winners

1933 — *Young Fu of the Upper Yangtze* by Elizabeth Foreman Lewis (Winston)
1943 — *Adam of the Road* by Elizabeth Janet Gray (Viking)
1944 — *Johnny Tremain* by Esther Forbes (Houghton)
1950 — *The Door in the Wall* by Marguerite de Angel (Doubleday)
1958 — *Rifles for Watie* by Harold Keith (Crowell)
1959 — *The Witch of Blackbird Pond* by Elizabeth George Speare (Houghton)
1961 — *Island of the Blue Dolphins* by Scott O'Dell (Houghton)

Carnegie Medal Winners

1951 — *Nicholas and the Wool-Pace* by Cynthia Harnett
1975 — *The Stronghold* by Mollie Hunter (Harper)

Canadian Library Association Award

1966 — *Raven's Cry* by Christie Harris (Atheneum)

I hope that you and your students will find the activities included in *And there I was . . .* valuable and enjoyable. As my Grandma Gussie, to whom this book is dedicated, would say, "So? What could be bad?"

Marji Gold-Vukson

Directions to the Student

1. Select an historic event from among the 29 presented in this book. Read the material accompanying the activity to gain a bit of insight into the event.

2. Locate additional information about the event. Record your findings on the lines provided for that purpose on the first page of the activity.

3. Select a "story starter" as directed on the second page of the activity. Place a checkmark by your selection.

4. Write a short story in the form of historical fiction on the lines provided. Be sure to base your story on the findings you recorded on the first page of the activity, as well as the information provided for you.

5. Your characters may be actual, historic personalities or those of your own creation. Strive to preserve the atmosphere *of the time* in your writing. (Descriptions of clothes, buildings, culture, food, language, etc., should be consistent.) For additional hints concerning research, ways to expand these activities, be sure to read A Few Hints below.

A Few Hints

1. Consider a *variety* of resources in your search to discover facts about the topics presented. While encyclopedias may often seem to be the most concise and logical place to start, you may wish to challenge yourself to avoid such sources by restricting yourself to primary printed sources only. (A primary resource is the original one: for instance, a newspaper story about an event.) Remember also, that your research may extend beyond your local library. Grandparents and other people, museums, archives, universities, interlibrary loans, and newspaper morgues, can make excellent resources, too.

2. Look beyond the facts. Investigate trends, attitudes, related events, and other factors which may have influenced the general climate of the time. Being aware of other underlying factors will not only help you to understand how and why the events came about, but will help you to develop more fully the elements (plot, characters, setting) of your short story, as well.

3. Feel free to enjoy greater flexibility with these activities by experimenting with alterations. For example, perhaps you wish to show how the events five years prior to a given situation led up to that situation. Changing the initial wording of the activity (from "The year was 1944" to "The year was 1939," for instance) and writing your own *story starter* in the space provided, might be one way to do this.

4. Consider expanding upon these activities. Perhaps your short story could be illustrated or made into a play. Maybe it could serve as the basis for a display, flannel board tale, or computer game. It might be enlightening to look at your findings about these events from the past and make some predictions about (or suggestions for) the future. This might even produce an appropriate "jumping off point" for a class debate. As you can see, the possibilities for expanding upon the activities here go on and on.

The year was 1902
Rudyard Kipling's Just So Stories

Rudyard Kipling, an English writer, was born in Bombay, India, in 1865. Most of his writings dealt with aspects of British colonial expansion into foreign countries. Among his writings are *Wee Willie Winkie and Other Stories* (1889), *The Jungle Book* (1894), *Captains Courageous* (1897), and *Ballads*, which includes "Fuzzy-Wuzzy." In 1902, Kipling wrote the *Just So Stories*, which explain such things as how the camel got its hump, how the elephant got its trunk, and how the whale got its throat.

What else can you discover about Rudyard Kipling, his *Just So Stories*, and the year 1902? Write your findings on the lines below:

_____
_____
_____
_____
_____
_____
_____
_____
_____
_____
_____
_____
_____
_____
_____
_____
_____
_____

(Please use additional paper for your research, if necessary.)

Write a short story beginning with one of the two prepared *story starters* below. (If you would prefer, you may compose your own original *story starter* in the space provided.)

_____ The year was 1902, and there I was, stumbling through the jungles of India, when I ran into . . .

_____ The year was 1902, and there I was, picnicking at the zoo and wondering how in the world that old elephant got its trunk, when . . .

_____ The year was 1902, and there I was _____

(Please use additional paper for your story, if necessary.)

The year was 1903
The Wright Brothers' First Flight

Wilbur (1867-1912) and Orville (1871-1948) Wright were interested in mechanics from the time they were very young. Inspired by what they read about Otto Lilienthal, a pioneer glider, they began to learn as much as possible about aeronautics. On December 17, 1903, they successfully flew an airplane they had invented and built. Although the flight lasted only 12 seconds and the plane flew only 120 feet, history was made that day.

What else can you discover about the Wright brothers, early aeronautics, and the year 1903? Write your findings on the lines below:

_____
_____
_____
_____
_____
_____
_____
_____
_____
_____
_____
_____
_____
_____
_____
_____
_____
_____

(Please use additional paper for your research, if necessary.)

Write a short story beginning with one of the two prepared *story starters* below. (If you would prefer, you may compose your own original *story starter* in the space provided.)

_____ The year was 1903, and there I was, waiting for the tire on my bicycle to be repaired, when I overheard . . .

_____ The year was 1903, and there I was, walking along the North Carolina shoreline one chilly December day, when I observed . .

_____ The year was 1903, and there I was _____

(Please use additional paper for your story, if necessary.)

— 7 —

The year was 1909

Robert Edwin Peary's Expedition North

Robert Edwin Peary became interested in exploring the Arctic regions after a trip he made into Greenland. After two "false starts" (one in 1897 and one in 1905), Peary and five assistants reached the North Pole on April 6, 1909. The United States Congress credited Peary with the discovery of the North Pole despite claims that another explorer reached the pole first.

What else can you discover about Robert Peary, early expeditions to the North Pole, and the year 1909? Write your findings on the lines below:

_____
_____
_____
_____
_____
_____
_____
_____
_____
_____
_____
_____
_____
_____
_____
_____
_____
_____
_____
_____
_____
_____

(Please use additional paper for your research, if necessary.)

Write a short story beginning with one of the two prepared *story starters* below. (If you would prefer, you may compose your own original *story starter* in the space provided.)

_____ The year was 1909, and there I was, with a dozen huskies and nowhere to go . . .
_____ The year was 1909, and there I was in line at the travel agency, listening to the man in front of me whine, "Farther north, farther north" when the now-irate agent turned to him and suggested . . .
_____ The year was 1909, and there I was _____

(Please use additional paper for your story, if necessary.)

The year was 1909
Henry Ford's Assembly Line

Henry Ford, who established the Ford Motor Company in 1903, realized that his early cars were too expensive for many people to afford. In 1909, in an effort to reduce production costs, Ford and his executives devised an *assembly line* method of production. In this way, a moving conveyor belt delivered parts (in various stages of completion) to the stationary workers. With each worker completing a prescribed task, the automobile assembly time was cut from about 12.5 hours to 1.5 hours!

What else can you discover about Henry Ford, the assembly line, and the year 1909? Write your findings on the lines below:

(Please use additional paper for your research, if necessary.)

Write a short story beginning with one of the two prepared *story starters* below. (If you would prefer, you may compose your own original *story starter* in the space provided.)

____ The year was 1909, and there I was, saying to my good friend, Henry, "I'll bet you that I can crank out a bunch of cars faster than you can" when, suddenly, he jumped to his feet, shouted "Eureka!" and . . .

____ The year was 1909, and there I was, in Dr. Frankenstein's laboratory, contemplating ways to adapt Henry Ford's assembly method, when . . .

____ The year was 1909, and there I was _____

(Please use additional paper for your story, if necessary.)

The year was 1912
The Unsinkable Titantic

The British steamer *Titanic* was the largest ship in the world when it was built. One night, during its very first voyage, the *Titanic* collided with an iceberg. There were not enough lifeboats to accommodate everyone. Of the approximately 2,200 passengers and crew aboard, only 705 survived when the "unsinkable" *Titanic* sank.

What else can you discover about the *Titanic*, early 20th century sea travel, and the year 1912? Write your findings on the lines below:

_____
_____
_____
_____
_____
_____
_____
_____
_____
_____
_____
_____
_____
_____
_____
_____
_____
_____
_____

(Please use additional paper for your research, if necessary.)

Write a short story beginning with one of the two prepared *story starters* below. (If you would prefer, you may compose your own original *story starter* in the space provided.)

_____ The year was 1912, and there I was, at the docks, trying to decide which ship to take to America, when . . .
_____ The year was 1912, and there I was, asking the purser where I might find a little more ice, when suddenly . . .
_____ The year was 1912, and there I was _____

(Please use additional paper for your story, if necessary.)

The year was 1912
Hans Geiger's Radiation Detector

Hans Geiger was a German physicist. In 1912, he invented an instrument to detect radiation. The Geiger Counter he invented "announced" the presence of radioactive materials such as uranium and thorium.

What else can you discover about Hans Geiger, the Geiger Counter, and the year 1912? Write your findings on the lines below:

_____
_____
_____
_____
_____
_____
_____
_____
_____
_____
_____
_____
_____
_____
_____
_____
_____
_____
_____

(Please use additional paper for your research, if necessary.)

Write a short story beginning with one of the two prepared *story starters* below. (If you would prefer, you may compose your own original *story starter* in the space provided.)

_____ The year was 1912, and there I was, glowing in the dark, when . . .
_____ The year was 1912, and there I was, working in my lab, when in walked a prospector with the remarkable proposition . . .
_____ The year was 1912, and there I was _____

(Please use additional paper for your story, if necessary.)

The year was 1914

The Panama Canal—Open for Business

The Panama Canal, which required $380 million and 10 years to build, is a 50.72 mile waterway linking the Atlantic and Pacific Oceans. Prior to the opening of the canal in 1914, ships travelling from New York to San Francisco had to go completely around South America!

What else can you discover about the construction of the Panama Canal and the year 1914? Write your findings on the lines below:

_____
_____
_____
_____
_____
_____
_____
_____
_____
_____
_____
_____
_____
_____
_____
_____
_____
_____
_____
_____
_____

(Please use additional paper for your research, if necessary.)

Write a short story beginning with one of the two prepared *story starters* below. (If you would prefer, you may compose your own original *story starter* in the space provided.)

_____ The year was 1914, and there I was, up to my hip-boots in mosquitoes, not feeling at all well, when . . .

_____ The year was 1914, and there I was, lounging on the deck and jotting down a few ideas for things to do once we disembarked in San Francisco, when . . .

_____ The year was 1914, and there I was _____

(Please use additional paper for your story, if necessary.)

—17—

The year was 1919

Mahatma Means Great Soul

Mohandas Karamchand Gandhi (1869-1948) was called Mahatma (Great Soul) by his followers in the Indian nationalist movement. He strongly believed that conflicts could be resolved by nonviolent means, that people should be tolerant of others, and that India should be free from British control. Gandhi demonstrated his positions on these issues with a campaign of fasting and nonviolent resistance that began in 1919.

What else can you discover about Mahatma Gandhi and the year 1919? Write your findings on the lines below:

(Please use additional paper for your research, if necessary.)

Write a short story beginning with one of the two prepared *story starters* below. (If you would prefer, you may compose your own original *story starter* in the space provided.)

_____ The year was 1919, and there I was, listening with the crowd to the Mahatma, when suddenly my stomach began to growl and . . .

_____ The year was 1919, and there I was with my regiment, fresh over from England, when . . .

_____ The year was 1919, and there I was _____

(Please use additional paper for your story, if necessary.)

The year was 1919

Temperance

The 18th amendment to the United States Constitution is the only one in history to have been repealed. The 18th amendment, which was ratified in 1919 and went into effect in 1920, prohibited the manufacture, sale, transportation, import, and export of beverages containing at least 0.5 percent alcohol; that is, liquor.

What else can you discover about the 18th amendment and the years 1919 and 1920? Write your findings on the lines below:

(Please use additional paper for your research, if necessary.)

Write a short story beginning with one of the two prepared *story starters* below. (If you would prefer, you may compose your own original *story starter* in the space provided.)

_____ The year was 1919, and there I was, in the lawyer's office, for the reading of the will through which I was to inherit my grandfather's winery, when . . .

_____ The year was 1920, and there I was, innocently sitting in this quaint little coffee house, when suddenly a barrage of police whistles . . .

_____ The year was 1919 or 1920, and there I was _____

(Please use additional paper for your story, if necessary.)

The year was 1925
John Baird's T.V.

If you are a couch potato, you can thank John Logie Baird. He was the Scottish engineer who invented television in 1925.

What else can you discover about John Logie Baird, early TV, and the year 1925? Write your findings on the lines below:

_____
_____
_____
_____
_____
_____
_____
_____
_____
_____
_____
_____
_____
_____
_____
_____
_____
_____

(Please use additional paper for your research, if necessary.)

___ The year was 1925, and there I was, sitting in the dark as I did every night, just watching the radio . . .
___ The year was 1925, and there I was waiting in the grocery line, when my friend, John Baird, spotting a new magazine called *TV Guide,* shouted, "There's a need to be filled here!" and . . .
___ The year was 1925, and there I was _____

_____
_____
_____
_____
_____
_____
_____
_____
_____
_____
_____
_____
_____
_____
_____

(Please use additional paper for your story, if necessary.)

The year was 1927
Charles Lindbergh's Nonstop Flight

Charles Augustus Lindbergh ("Lone Eagle") was the first aviator to fly nonstop across the Atlantic Ocean. He made the flight as the result of an offer made by a wealthy hotel owner, Raymond Orteig, in 1919. Orteig promised $25,000 to the first aviator to fly from New York to Paris, nonstop. In May of 1927, almost eight years after the offer was made, Lindbergh flew the *Spirit of St. Louis* from Roosevelt Field in New York to Le Bourget Field in Paris. The flight set a record at 20 hours and 21 minutes.

What else can you discover about Charles Lindbergh, his flight in the *Spirit of St. Louis*, and the year 1927? Write your findings on the lines below:

_____
_____
_____
_____
_____
_____
_____
_____
_____
_____
_____
_____
_____
_____
_____
_____
_____
_____
_____

(Please use additional paper for your research, if necessary.)

_____ The year was 1927, and there I was, a cub reporter with the *Picayune de Paris*, standing at Bourget Field in hopes of a big break, when . . .

_____ The year was 1927, and there I was, listening to the radio with my good friend, Raymond, when suddenly . . .

_____ The year was 1927, and there I was _____

(Please use additional paper for your story, if necessary.)

The year was 1929
Black Thursday

In the mid to late 1920s, the value of common stocks on the New York Stock Exchange rose dramatically. Hoping to make money, people began to buy stocks on speculation. They expected the value of the stocks to continue to rise. Unfortunately, on October 24, 1929 ("Black Thursday"), stock values plummetted. They continued to fall on the following Monday, and, on Tuesday, the frightened stockholders quickly sold a record 16,410,030 shares of stock. The stock was no longer worth its original purchase price. Banks, businesses, and individuals found themselves in financial ruin as the stock market crashed.

What else can you discover about the Stock Market Crash, the Great Depression, and the year 1929? Write your findings on the lines below:

(Please use additional paper for your research, if necessary.)

_____ The year was 1929, and there I was, gazing out of my Wall Street window at the ledge across from mine when, to my horror, . . .

_____ The year was 1929, and there I was with a portfolio of worthless stock certificates, thinking to myself . . .

_____ The year was 1929, and there I was _____

(Please use additional paper for your story, if necessary.)

—27—

The year was 1936
A Royal Love Story

King Edward VIII was the son of King George V and Queen Mary of Great Britain. In the 1930s, he fell in love with an American woman named Wallis Warfield Simpson. Mrs. Simpson was a *"commoner"* and a divorcee. For these and other reasons, King Edward's government refused to accept her as queen. As a result, Edward abdicated his throne on December 11, 1936, left England, and married Mrs. Simpson. In 1940, George VI, who succeeded his brother to the throne, made Edward governor of the Bahamas.

What else can you discover about King Edward VIII, his romance, and the year 1936? Write your findings on the lines below:

_____
_____
_____
_____
_____
_____
_____
_____
_____
_____
_____
_____
_____
_____
_____
_____
_____
_____
_____
_____

(Please use additional paper for your research, if necessary.)

Write a short story beginning with one of the two prepared *story starters* below. (If you would prefer, you may compose your own original *story starter* in the space provided.)

_____ The year was 1936, and there I was, in my final year of Parliament, when a most distressing situation concerning King Edward . . .

_____ The year was 1936, and there I was, standing behind the counter of my small bridal boutique, when who should walk in but . . .

_____ The year was 1936, and there I was _____

(Please use additional paper for your story, if necessary.)

The year was 1939
Good as Mold

Penicillin was discovered in 1928 by the British scientist, Sir Alexander Fleming. He noticed that mold of the genus penicillium, growing around bacteria in a laboratory dish, had apparently killed the bacteria. Unfortunately, in further experiments, Fleming had a hard time removing the mold from the substance in which it was grown. About 10 years later, Howard Florey and Ernst Chain found a way to extract and purify penicillin. Penicillin was fully developed in 1939 and by the 1940s was used as an antibiotic to treat diseases in humans.

What else can you discover about penicillin, the scientists who played parts in its discovery and refinement, and the year 1939? Write your findings on the lines below:

(Please use additional paper for your research, if necessary.)

Write a short story beginning with one of the two prepared *story starters* below. (If you would prefer, you may compose your own original *story starter* in the space provided.)

_____ The year was 1939, and there I was, griping to my colleague, Alex, about his shoddy work habits which allowed mold to grow all over my bacteria experiment, when . . .

_____ The year was 1939, and there I was, with about a half pound of garlic tied around my neck and a gallon of chicken soup on the stove, when . . .

_____ The year was 1939, and there I was _____

(Please use additional paper for your story, if necessary.)

—31—

The year was 1944
Anne Frank's Secret Place

For over two years during World War II, Anne Frank and her family hid in the attic in Amsterdam. On August 4, 1944, they were seized by the Nazis and taken to concentration camps. At the end of the war, Anne's father, the only surviving member of the family, returned to the attic and found the diary that Anne had begun on her 13th birthday. *The Diary of Anne Frank*, which reflects extraordinary courage and optimism in the face of adversity, has now been translated into 40 languages and read by over 60 million people.

What else can you discover about Anne Frank, the Holocaust, and the year 1944? Write your findings on the lines below:

(Please use additional paper for your research, if necessary.)

Write a short story beginning with one of the two prepared *story starters* below. (If you would prefer, you may compose your own original *story starter* in the space provided.)

_____ The year was 1944, and there I was in the Amsterdam office, when, from overhead, came the faint, but unmistakable sounds of . . .

_____ The year was 1944, and there I was, exhausted, but, as ever, too frightened to sleep, when I saw them bring in the young girl, named Anne, who . . .

_____ The year was 1944, and there I was _____

(Please use additional paper for your story, if necessary.)

— 33 —

The year was 1945
Hiroshima and Nagasaki

On August 6, 1945, the United States dropped a gun-type fission bomb on the city of Hiroshima, Japan. The bomb killed 70 to 100 thousand people almost immediately. On August 9, 1945, an implosion-type fission bomb was dropped on Nagasaki, Japan. About 40 thousand people died. Many other people later died from the injuries and radiation caused by the dropping of these two bombs.

What else can you discover about atomic bombs, the attacks on Hiroshima and Nagasaki, and the year 1945? Write your findings on the lines below:

_____
_____
_____
_____
_____
_____
_____
_____
_____
_____
_____
_____
_____
_____
_____
_____
_____
_____
_____

(Please use additional paper for your research, if necessary.)

Write a short story beginning with one of the two prepared *story starters* below. (If you would prefer, you may compose your own original *story starter* in the space provided.)

_____ The year was 1945, and there I was, at the market in my little village, not twenty kilometers from Hiroshima, when I felt . . .
_____ The year was 1945, and there I was, high in the air over Nagasaki, thinking to myself . . .
_____ The year was 1945, and there I was _____

_____
_____
_____
_____
_____
_____
_____
_____
_____
_____
_____
_____
_____
_____
_____
_____
_____
_____
_____
_____
_____
_____
_____
_____
_____

(Please use additional paper for your story, if necessary.)

The year was 1947
A Sonic Boom

The word *supersonic* refers to speeds greater than the speed of sound. Supersonic flight occurs when an aircraft flies faster than the speed of sound. The first supersonic flight was made by a rocket-powered plane in the year 1947.

What else can you discover about the first and subsequent supersonic flights and the year 1947? Write your findings on the lines below:

_____
_____
_____
_____
_____
_____
_____
_____
_____
_____
_____
_____
_____
_____
_____
_____
_____
_____
_____
_____
_____
_____
_____

(Please use additional paper for your research, if necessary.)

Write a short story beginning with one of the two prepared *story starters* below. (If you would prefer, you may compose your own original *story starter* in the space provided.)

_____ The year was 1947, and there I was waiting at the airbase, quite anxious about my sure-to-be-history-making flight, when . . .

_____ The year was 1947, and there I was napping in my hammock, when a horrible, nerve-wracking, window-shattering BOOM . . .

_____ The year was 1947, and there I was _____

(Please use additional paper for your story, if necessary.)

— 37 —

The year was 1950
One for All and All for One—NATO

The North Atlantic Treaty Organization (NATO) was established in 1950. It was created to insure that its 16-member nations from the West would come to each other's aid in case one or more of them was ever attacked by aggressive forces from outside the alliance.

What else can you discover about NATO, its members, and the year 1950? Write your findings on the lines below:

(Please use additional paper for your research, if necessary.)

Write a short story beginning with one of the two prepared *story starters* below. (If you would prefer, you may compose your own original *story starter* in the space provided.)

_____ The year was 1950, and there I was, hoping that the newly formed Western alliance — NATO — which my country had recently joined, . . .

_____ The year was 1950, and there I was, with my comrades, discussing how insulting it was of the Western nations to form a new alliance against us in *peacetime*, when . . .

_____ The year was 1950, and there I was _____

(Please use additional paper for your story, if necessary.)

The year was 1956
Deposit Another Dime, Please

Many advancements in technology have taken place since the first underground telephone cable was installed in 1902. Tubes, amplifiers, transistors, fiber-optics, and improved cables have all played a part in improving communication by telephone. In 1956, the first transatlantic cable, extending from Newfoundland to Scotland, was put into place. After all of these years, the cable is still in existence!

What else can you discover about the first transatlantic telephone cable, the impact it had on the world, and the year 1956? Write your findings on the lines below:

(Please use additional paper for your research, if necessary.)

Write a short story beginning with one of the two prepared *story starters* below. (If you would prefer, you may compose your own original *story starter* in the space provided.)

_____ The year was 1956, and there I was, struggling to unreel the massive cable into the ocean, when I realized . . .

_____ The year was 1956, and there I was, on the phone shouting, "Hello? Hello?" when, would you believe it, . . .

_____ The year was 1956, and there I was _____

(Please use additional paper for your story, if necessary.)

—41—

The year was 1958
Bobby Fischer and the Big Checkmate

Bobby Fischer enjoyed playing chess from the time he was very young. In 1958, when he was just 14 years old, Fischer won his first United States chess championship. The next year, he became an international grand master of chess — the youngest person ever to have done so!

What else can you discover about Bobby Fischer, the history of his chess career, and the year 1958? Write your findings on the lines below:

(Please use additional paper for your research, if necessary.)

Write a short story beginning with one of the two prepared *story starters* below. (If you would prefer, you may compose your own original *story starter* in the space provided.)

_____ The year was 1958, and there I was, with only 20 seconds left on the clock, no obvious strategy in mind, and Bobby's voice echoing loudly in my head, "CHECK!" when . . .

_____ The year was 1958, and there I was, rather unenthusiastic about the new chess board I had just received, when I heard a rumor that a boy named Bobby, who was just a couple of years older than myself . . .

_____ The year was 1958, and there I was _____

(Please use additional paper for your story, if necessary.)

The year was 1960
J.F.K., The Nation's Youngest President

In 1960, when John F. Kennedy was elected to the office of President of the United States, he became the youngest person ever to have done so. John Kennedy was 43. With his assassination three years later, Kennedy became the youngest president to die in office, as well.

What else can you discover about John F. Kennedy, his administration, and the years 1960-63? Write your findings on the lines below:

(Please use additional paper for your research, if necessary.)

Write a short story beginning with one of the two prepared *story starters* below. (If you would prefer, you may compose your own original *story starter* in the space provided.)

_____ The year was 1960, and there I was at Mass, when the priest proudly announced . . .
_____ The year was 1960, and there I was, back at the Republican headquarters, when . . .
_____ The year was 1960, and there I was _____

(Please use additional paper for your story, if necessary.)

— 45 —

The year was 1963
Valentina Tereshkova—Out of This World

Russian cosmonaut, Valentina Vladimirovna Tereshkova, was the first woman to travel in space. Her flight, in a spacecraft called *Vostok VI*, lasted from June 16 to June 19, 1963. Unlike her predecessors, Tereshkova had no previous experience as a test pilot. She had pursued parachuting as a hobby, however. This was fortunate, since Tereshkova was required to parachute to Earth from the *Vostok VI* at the end of her journey!

What else can you discover about Valentina Tereshkova, the *Vostok VI*, and the year 1963? Write your findings on the lines below:

_____
_____
_____
_____
_____
_____
_____
_____
_____
_____
_____
_____
_____
_____
_____
_____
_____
_____
_____
_____
_____

(Please use additional paper for your research, if necessary.)

Write a short story beginning with one of the two prepared *story starters* below. (If you would prefer, you may compose your own original *story starter* in the space provided.)

_____ The year was 1963, and there I was, with my friend and professional rival, Valentina, when the head of the space agency announced . . .

_____ The year was 1963, and there I was, on the deck of my boat, watching the sea birds when, from out of the skies . . .

_____ The year was 1963, and there I was _____

(Please use additional paper for your story, if necessary.)

The year was 1968
Martin Luther King, Robert F. Kennedy

The year 1968 saw the assassinations of two young American leaders. The first was that of civil rights leader, Martin Luther King. He was shot and killed on April 4 in Memphis, TN, where he had gone to support a strike of black garbage collectors. The second was that of Robert F. Kennedy, former attorney general and United States senator. He was campaigning for the Democratic nomination for President of the United States when, in June of the year, he was shot and killed.

What else can you discover about Martin Luther King, Robert F. Kennedy, and the year 1968? Write your findings on the lines below:

(Please use additional paper for your research, if necessary.)

Write a short story beginning with one of the two prepared *story starters* below. (If you would prefer, you may compose your own original *story starter* in the space provided.)

_____ The year was 1968, and there I was, deep in thought, when I began to dream . . .
_____ The year was 1968, and there I was, in the midst of the primary victory celebration in Los Angeles, almost close enough to touch Bobby, when the sound of . . .
_____ The year was 1968, and there I was _____

(Please use additional paper for your story, if necessary.)

The year was 1976
A Mysterious Illness—Legionnaires' Disease

In July of 1976, 221 people attending an American Legion convention in Philadelphia, PA, suddenly became ill with a mysterious disease. They experienced fever, coughing, chest pain, and difficulty in breathing. When it was over, 34 of those stricken had died. The illness was called "Legionnaires' Disease." Not until January, 1977, were scientists able to determine that the cause of the disease was an unusual pneumonia-causing bacteria. The bacteria was later named *Legionella pneumophila*.

What else can you discover about Legionnaires' Disease, the American Legion convention, and the year 1976? Write your findings on the lines below:

_____
_____
_____
_____
_____
_____
_____
_____
_____
_____
_____
_____
_____
_____
_____
_____
_____
_____

(Please use additional paper for your research, if necessary.)

Write a short story beginning with one of the two prepared *story starters* below. (If you would prefer, you may compose your own original *story starter* in the space provided.)

_____ The year was 1976, and there I was, in the restaurant of a Philadelphia hotel, beginning to feel rather dizzy, when a frightened Legionnaire at the next table told me . . .

_____ The year was 1976, and there I was, in my first year with the Philadelphia Department of Tourism, when into my office rushed a panic-stricken public health officer shouting . . .

_____ The year was 1976, and there I was _____

(Please use additional paper for your story, if necessary.)

The year was 1978
A $2,000,000 Bible

Over 500 years ago, Johannes Gutenberg invented a special mold which allowed movable metallic type to be used successfully in printing. With help from his colleagues, Fust and Schoeffer, Gutenberg perfected the process of typography. His printing press was a precision instrument and was used in the printing of many fine works. One such item was the Gutenberg Bible. In 1978, a Gutenberg Bible sold at auction in New York for $2 million.

What else can you discover about the history of the printing press, the Gutenberg Bible, and the year 1978? Write your findings on the lines below:

_____
_____
_____
_____
_____
_____
_____
_____
_____
_____
_____
_____
_____
_____
_____
_____
_____
_____
_____

(Please use additional paper for your research, if necessary.)

Write a short story beginning with one of the two prepared *story starters* below. (If you would prefer, you may compose your own original *story starter* in the space provided.)

_____ The year was 1978, and there I was, swatting at the fly who was buzzing by my head, when, to my great surprise, the auctioneer smiled in my direction, slammed down his gavel, pronounced the $2 million Bible Sold! and I knew . . .

_____ The year was 1978, and there I was, following the auctioning off of the Gutenberg Bible for $2 million and thinking that if *I* had that kind of money, I would . . .

_____ The year was 1978, and there I was _____

(Please use additional paper for your story, if necessary.)

— 53 —

The year was 1978
The Return of Susan B. Anthony

Susan Brownell Anthony (1820-1906) was one of the early leaders in the movement for women's rights. Although she worked hard to secure the right for women to vote, the 19th amendment giving women that right was not ratified until 14 years after her death. On October 10, 1978, the United States Congress honored the memory of Susan B. Anthony and her work by authorizing the minting of Susan B. Anthony coins. The first such copper/nickel-clad dollar was minted in Philadelphia in December, 1978. The last was minted in 1981.

What else can you discover about Susan B. Anthony, the Susan B. Anthony coin, and the year 1978? Write your findings on the lines below:

(Please use additional paper for your research, if necessary.)

Write a short story beginning with one of the two prepared *story starters* below. (If you would prefer, you may compose your own original *story starter* in the space provided.)

_____ The year was 1978, and there I was, clumsily trying to retrieve the $3 worth of Susan B. Anthony coins that I had accidentally dropped into the coin box instead of quarters, when the irate bus passengers in line behind me . . .

_____ The year was 1978, and there I was, waiting for word as to whether or not the new Susan B. Anthony coin . . .

_____ The year was 1978, and there I was _____

(Please use additional paper for your story, if necessary.)

The year was 1982
A Heart Called Jarvik-7

Experimentation with artificial hearts made of materials such as plastic, titanium, and carbon began as early as 1957. These hearts were tested in calves and other animals. In 1982, Dr. William DeVries led a team of surgeons in the implantation of an artificial heart, the Jarvik-7, in a human patient named Barney B. Clark. Clark survived for almost four months. Many people considered the 1982 implant to be the first successful permanent artificial heart operation.

What else can you discover about artificial hearts, Barney Clark's surgery, Dr. William DeVries, and the year 1982? Write your findings on the lines below:

(Please use additional paper for your research, if necessary.)

Write a short story beginning with one of the two prepared *story starters* below. (If you would prefer, you may compose your own original *story starter* in the space provided.)

_____ The year was 1982, and there I was in my fourth year of medical school, when Dr. William DeVries addressed the class and announced . . .

_____ The year was 1982, and there I was visiting Barney Clark almost eight weeks after his surgery, when I realized . . .

_____ The year was 1982, and there I was _____

(Please use additional paper for your story, if necessary.)

The year was 1986
Voyager II and the Ten New Moons

Uranus is the seventh planet from the sun. Until recently, it was believed that five satellites (moons) orbited the planet. These five were first noticed in the period from 1787 to 1948. When the United States spacecraft *Voyager II* passed the planet in 1986, however, 10 additional moons were detected!

What else can you discover about Uranus, *Voyager II*, and the year 1986? Write your findings on the lines below:

_____
_____
_____
_____
_____
_____
_____
_____
_____
_____
_____
_____
_____
_____
_____
_____
_____
_____
_____
_____

(Please use additional paper for your research, if necessary.)

Write a short story beginning with one of the two prepared *story starters* below. (If you would prefer, you may compose your own original *story starter* in the space provided.)

_____ The year was 1986, and there I was staring at the monitor in disbelief as the *Voyager II* beamed back a series of pictures that appeared to indicate . . .
_____ The year was 1986, and there I was, feeling a bit like a proud new parent, as the *Voyager II* . . .
_____ The year was 1986, and there I was _____

(Please use additional paper for your story, if necessary.)

The year was 1989
A Hero Named Secretariat

In the midst of Watergate and Vietnam, America needed a hero. With his *Triple Crown* win in 1973, a young race horse by the name of Secretariat provided one. Secretariat easily won the Kentucky Derby and the Preakness, but it was his 31 length (6.15 second) victory in the Belmont Stakes that made him the first Triple Crown winner in a quarter of a century. Sadly, on Labor Day of 1989, a veterinarian found laminitis, an incurable inflammation, inside of Secretariat's hoof. On October 4, 1989, he was put to sleep. The 19-year-old chestnut hero was buried near his father, Bold Ruler, and his grandfather, Nasrullah, at the Clairborne Farm in Paris, KY.

What else can you discover about Secretariat, the Triple Crown, horse care, and the years 1973 and 1989? Write your findings on the lines below:

(Please use additional paper for your research, if necessary.)

Write a short story beginning with one of the two prepared *story starters* below. (If you would prefer, you may compose your own original *story starter* in the space provided.)

_____ The year was 1989, and there I was, just horsing around in the barn, when the veterinarian somberly approached my stall and . . .

_____ The year was 1989, and there I was in Paris, KY, enjoying a lovely Labor Day picnic, when . . .

_____ The year was 1989, and there I was _____

_____
_____
_____
_____
_____
_____
_____
_____
_____
_____
_____
_____
_____
_____
_____
_____
_____
_____

(Please use additional paper for your story, if necessary.)